for Evelyn Stachel,
best wishes,
Charlotte Mandel

Also by Charlotte Mandel

Keeping Him Alive

The Life of Mary

Doll

A Disc of Clear Water

Saturday's Women (Editor,
with Maxine Silverman
and Rachel Hadas)

The Marriages of Jacob

A POEM–NOVELLA

Charlotte Mandel

MICAH PUBLICATIONS

ACKNOWLEDGEMENTS:
I am grateful to Villa Montalvo Center for the Arts
and to the Corporation of Yaddo for providing tran-
quility and place for uninterrupted concentration,
and to the Geraldine E. Dodge Foundation which
sponsored my residence at Yaddo. To Dr. Yael
Feldman, my deep appreciation for allowing me to
benefit from her course, "The Bible as Literature", at
Columbia University. For translation of names, *In
the Beginning: A New English Translation of the Book of
Genesis* by Everett Fox (New York: Schocken Books,
1983) has been an inspiring source.

Typesetting by The Geryon Press, Limited.

Cover design by Robert and Roberta Kalechofsky.

Library of Congress Cataloging-in-Publication Data

Mandel, Charlotte
    The marriages of Jacob : a poem-novella / Charlotte Mandel.
        p.   cm.
      ISBN 0-916288-32-3 (acid-free paper)
      1. Jacob (Biblical patriarch)—Poetry. 2. Bible. O.T.—History
of Biblical events—Poetry. I. Title.
PS3563.A4358M3 1991
811' .54—dc20
                                                            91-10855
                                                            CIP

MICAH PUBLICATIONS
255 Humphrey Street
Marblehead, MA 01945

For Manny,

our children,

and grandchildren

Part One

I

Silence veils this bride
no less than her lowered hood
sewn with seven stems of silver wheat

Seven years this virgin groom
has buried his fists in her father's harvests,
bound sheep's wool into humps

A bargain—the heat of his body
for the fragrance of Rachel,
Laban's daughter.
                    A swollen moon,
thorned stars and fruitful vines
pattern the roof of the wedding tent

loomed by the hummingbird fingers
of girls too young to have bled.
Her bearded brothers are grinning

with closed lips at their father's wit:
"Did he not ask
for my daughter, and do I not give him

my daughter Leah?"

II

Rachel unravels her braids,
head tilted to the distant marriage cry
of flutes, the tambourines' applause.

Her skin glistening in the sweaty twilight,
she sits crosslegged on the sisters' bed,
loosens her white shift.
Arms dancing with the snakes of her hair

she rolls her small belly. . .whispers
"Leah, Jacob, be thou
my wife, my husband," opening her knees

she twines herself around the wedding music,
hearing the beat of Jacob's heart upon Leah's,
feeling his hand over their similar breasts,
over navel and hips wider
than her own. All night, the harp
quivers outside the wedding tent
where Jacob lies with Leah

breathing the name of Rachel
who knows the warmth of Leah

(each day, as mirror to the other,
breasts touching, weaving
one another's hair

braiding the near strands
into one thick plait
to sleep entwined in the dark
shining chain)

III

Jacob spindles into the flash
of sun rising, his ram's horns
tearing the wool of whirling clouds,
nostrils inhaling the musk
of a thousand ewes.
Clouds mist

clear drops over the earth
and to the farthest circle of the world
his flock sways silver and endless
as a sea. From the mountain peak

his horned head lowers to Rachel
far, far in the field,
she grasps the twin spirals of bone
up to his side,
yet she cleaves into two,
herself and herself,
each with an arm
drawn through the crook of a crescent horn.

IV

Leah listens to the night
letting go of the world,
rippling throats of doves,
heads hidden under wings

Jacob's arm
wooden as the yoke she bears
from the well

the flail of his ribs
draws the air from her chest
(Sister, your breath
still a child's and mine
forever pressed into the moans
of a woman
do you hear our mother?

gray light
afterglow

will my blood
appease him?

Dawn and the canopy's stars turn
white as claws

V

In the festival tent, Laban
hoists a filled sheep's belly of wine
to the next of his sons in the kinsmen's
ring of open red mouths.
The lamps' sweet oils have thickened
to sandalwood smoke.

Dull with half-sleep, hooded, swathed
in muted colors, the women sit apart,
backs touching woven walls.

Yet the men stagger up once more,
arms upon shoulders, chanting
to tireless palms on drum, shuffle
of white robes becoming one
body of the father, a torso
with many quick feet.

Softly, the sandals rise and fall,
slowly, the ring turns.
Sunlight pours through the entrance.
Jacob stands barefoot,
the muscles of his neck swelling.

"Our son!"
the male body roars
embracing the bridegroom
with its hundred arms.

VI

Serpentine, the line of women
glides into morning, sandals
stir the waking village dust

Returning to the bridal tent, ritual
that echoes between thighs
like weeping too far to be heard

Women's hands pass like breezes
winnowing fronds of Leah's hair
still fragrant with oils of myrrh,
aloe, cinnamon

Four who have borne and suckled sons
sever from the circle,
take up the corners of the wedding sheet,
unfurl triumphant stains of stiffened blood

Left palm to the right of one,
right palm to the left of another,
circling the bride, voices
ullulating

Praise for the bridal cup
broken and mended
by marriage

Folded by the pattern of dance,
the wedding sheet will be burned,
ashes buried at the edge
of the wheat field—
her blood/his sperm

Ewers of sweet well water dissolve
traces of salt on Leah's cheeks,
dried flecks on her thighs

Now she is theirs
forever in the company of wives.

VII

Yet not a wife.
If Jacob will not fulfill
their bridal week,
she will be the mother
of barren seed
widow with no grave to mourn

daughter of no worth to her father
ewe born with three legs
camel blind in one eye
goat with sealed udders

sister torn from sister

a bride
deflowered

discarded

VIII

Who is Leah—one
of a swirl, clusters of giggling

at looms, domed ovens, bent
over clothes at the shallow river basin,

hands smelling of curds—
scuffling sandals—skirts in the wind—

Leah to Rachel is shadow
to its glittering gnomon

or nothing
for Jacob has not perceived her

IX

Leah's skin is smooth, olive dark
as Rachel's, her hair well burnished

but Rachel's eyes draw Jacob to the sounding
black of water deep in stone,
underground springs rushing
to ease his thirst

Leah's eyes shift like clouds
of pale gray haze
in a summer of drought

X

A man's fist draws back the tent's curtain.

Leah's eyes cast down to the prayer of her hands.

She hears his step and bows her head,
sees only his calloused feet.

She knows the ache beginning to dull
between her legs

and nothing else of her life.

XI

There is always hunger
and the hot bread.
The bride has milled this portion's flour
crouched on her knees to drive the stone,
kneaded yeast dough with her fists,
baked risen rounds upon the upraised belly
of the clay oven.

There is the wedding broth of milk,
beaten eggs and crushed almonds
sweetened with drops of date honey

the gift tray of woven reeds
set with Sumerian glazed bowls.

The bread and the broth steam to their nostrils.
A knot eases / another enters the weave /
Jacob the bondsman
eats Leah's bread.

XII

Jacob watches her deft
gold-brown fingers
nest the bowls
on the basket-tray—

"These are not wild meats,"
he says. "Your father needs to kill
only what belongs to him.
What of you, Leah?
Do you roast wild game?"
He stares with anger
into her pale blue eyes,
the hunter's eyes of redhaired Esau,
his brother.

XIII

Jacob's muscles tense against the wheel
of a great stone

as though bound like one of Laban's young
rams to be wrestled from a ewe in heat

and he nearly bursts free—
light on his toes, listening

to the steady scrape of sand as his wife
scours bowls outside the tent

Her scent rises from his own sweat
Virginal oils, blood and brine
cloud his skin

("Rachel," he had groaned to her, "Rachel")

He wants to dive into a desert dune
rake her sour-sweet dampness from his pores

and when she slips back into the tent
he lifts her by the waist

throws her to the carpet floor
thrusts into her
again and again
crying her name:
"Leah! Leah!"

XIV

Leah shrinks from Jacob's fists
clenched at the edge of his dream

where he wrestles naked
with another man, twin,
with hairy arms and chest

wrestling blind in the dark
of a tent buffeted by flails,
walls collapsing
hot upon their slippery sweat

Yet their lungs rest, calm
as the tent's walls beat
upon them
beating
thuds of rhythmic blows—

In the distance—
a highpitched
razoring scream
of a riven animal
or a woman

XV

The mountain's shadow descending
binds the village in early twilight

urging the flock to habits of the fold,
relief of milk drawn.

The sun, too, returns to its resting place.
On this moonless night, stars will swarm,

fireflies assemble
sudden constellations over fields.

Once, he came to his mother
with a lamp of living fire—

a winged beetle
saved in the keep of his child's hands.

Below, a constellation forms the sinewed
hook of Esau's bow.

Warm hairs of a young goat's flank
brush against his wrist

prickling, like his brother's skin,
like the young goat's hide draped

by Rebecca upon his neck and arms.
Jacob closes his eyes,

lets his fingers stumble like an aged man's
upon the bleating goat's flanks.

Are you he, his father asks, *my son Esau?*
Jacob answers, *I am.*

XVI

"Leah, how did your mother die?"

"After five sons and myself, first daughter,
she died at my sister's birth."

"Leah, for seven years, I have herded
your father's sheep. One ewe was promised to me—
your sister, whose name means 'ewe.'
Leah, your name signifies 'wild cow.'
Are you wild, Leah?
After these seven days, I will be husband
to one sheep, one cow.
Am I ram, then, or bull?

Am I foreigner or kin?
The bread of our neighbors in Canaan
folded like wool in the hands.
My mother's bread was harsh and brittle
like the breads of this household.
She is your father's sister, you my cousin-wife.
We are a family of brittle gifts."

"My father, Jacob, my father decides—"

"I have deserved this—I am Jacob which means
'heel-sneak'—born with my hand pulling the heel
of my firstborn twin.
Yet my brother's hunger rules without thought.
For a pot of red beans, he sold
his firstborn right, and it is mine.

Cook for me, Leah.
Here, we will fulfill your seven days."

XVII

A doubled house, clay walls
and roof of thatch. To each
a room and handmaid's niche,
to both the central hearth,
spinning skeins and loom,
potter's shelf and grinding stones.

Laban tallies his wealth in sons,
daughters and increase
of their households.
He owns the flocks and beasts of burden;
roots and stones of the wild pastures;
oxtrodden furrows for wheat, barley, lentils;
fig trees, olives, persimmons;
blades of green flax and skeins of linen;
potters' jugs, the fermenting beer;
unwashed humps of fleece and rolls
of spun dyed wool.

He owns the quick blur of weavers' fingers;
the leathery squinted lines that ray
from farseeing eyes of shepherds;
reapers' knotted backs, the dust and chaff
in their nostrils; their tents of goat hair
and rugs on beaten earth floors.

He owns the teraphim,
ancestral mother/father of his tribe,
the oracle skulls with eyes of agate.

XVIII

"Not every new wife has a handmaid—
Zilpah knows how to dye cloth—
look at the purple stripe in her dress—
the dye is made from shell
gathered in the tides off Cyprus
where she was born, the trader says.
But she speaks Aramean.
I chose her to match you
for her eyes—gray and pale—
as a child, you wept too much.

Doesn't this house prove
you have a good father?
You and Rachel will live as sisters forever.

Now, would it redden your eyes
to be a mother?
Give me grandsons
for as many years as grains of sand
from our village to the sea.
Then you'll be happy."

XIX

If Zilpah weeps, no one sees or hears.
Cleverness casts eyelids down.
Palms clasp, shell upon shell—like the blind
creatures she would harvest at ebb tide

until fires arrowed from the sea—
fishermen's roofs blazing—
the sacrificial smell
of oxen burning alive—

her father's curled fair beard
his mouth

the club
covered with blood and shreds
like offal of a slaughtered pig—

her limbs numbed in the cords
of her father's own net,
throat gasping, voiceless as a fish
under the soldier's arm,
ribs in pain against his—

tossed to the scummed slab
of a longnecked ship—
This mermaid's my catch!

But she has never walked beside a camel.
The trader at Mari gives fair value.
A bride's handmaid must be a virgin.

XX

Is she dolphin
or saddled rider
choking in undertow?
Tidal breakers crash
green waters ebb
steam gold   disappear
Lizards dart under stones
Zilpah wakes

beneath fragrant new thatch.
Her mistress sips from a bowl of water
boiled with thyme.

Crackle of fire
singeing hides of festival lamb and calf—
another ritual feast,
a daughter's wedding.

Tremble of boiling tea
scalds Leah's hands.
Since the day of Rachel's birth,
but for these seven nights,
the two have slept as twins.

Zilpah brings cool water.

XXI

Twin—but for Leah's silent gaze
and Rachel's laughter—a flute
edged with mockery like the quick
tambourine rattle of beads.

Rachel laughs to the mirror
she sees in her sister's love.
Leah loves
the self she cannot be.

If, when sleeping entwined by one plait,
turning her back one pulls
the other's hair, both waking in pain,

the sisters learn
how dreams may be
subdued to parallels.

XXII

Beyond the courtyard, Leah sees her sister
running to the fold with a new lamb

wet with birth in her arms—a twin
refused by its mother.

Rachel rubs the newborn's caul
to the nostrils of a sister ewe

about to wean her older lamb.
The scent pleases her,

and happily deceived,
she suckles the orphan.

XXIII

Imad's donkey trots faster toward
the valley wind's aroma of fruit
ripening on Laban's trees.
A long wake of dust
trails the sure, clicking hooves.
The man sniffs, and chants
invocation to the god of this wind,
for he inscribes amulets, talismanic rhymes,
prayers to many spirits.

Laban's tribe praises a god
whose name they hide,
sounds that have no alphabet.
The scribe records accounts:
harvest yield, livestock,
taxes, purchase and sale
of oil, wool, handmaid or bondsman,
agreed price of a bride.

XXIV

Striding across the courtyard
with a trumpeting laugh
and scything sweep of arm
to the women who stand
like shrouded urns in doorways,
Laban heralds Imad:

"The scribe has honored us—hurry—
pour water over his feet.
Bring fruit, cakes, tea!"

His eldest son helps the bald stooped guest
to dismount, others unsling the quiver
of tablet reeds and basket of wet clay
from the beast's matted withers,
tug its bridle
toward the drinking trough.

XXV

Overhead, wings of yellow bees
vibrate through tree shade.

In the scribe's hard palms, wet clay
forms a disc, stretches to a square.

Sparrow tracks race upon clay
as the tablet reed twirls up/down/across
in horizontal rows from right to left
recording syllables

while Laban dictates, and Jacob
watches his uncle's lips.
The scribe remembers the tablet
seven years past. Thereon
was promised *Laban's daughter*
to a youth whose cheeks glowed
silk as persimmons.
Now a dark beard defines his jaw.
The bridegroom's stole
covers shoulders
doubled in breadth.

The tablet reed engraves:

In the lambing month, 14th day,
18 years following the accession of Zumi,
Jacob son of Isaac has fulfilled his bridal
with Leah daughter of Laban son of Betuel.
This same day Jacob takes for wife
Rachel daughter of Laban son of Betuel

The scribe turns the moist clay square
over onto its back.
The reed engraves:

in price of which he promises
service to her father seven years to come.
In seal thereof Jacob son of Isaac
and Laban son of Betuel have affixed
the imprint of their thumbnails.
Witnessed by Imad the scribe.

By sundown, the tablet with two sides
will register in baked stone
the marriages of Jacob.

XXVI

Bell, harp and tambourine
accompany the wedding feast.

Under the new roof, Zilpah silently
soothes the old wife's ravelled braid
with a comb of polished olivewood,
fashions a snail shell spiral
above her outstretched nape.
Leah is comforted and takes her hand.

"Zilpah, here, sit in front of me.
Look up—
look at my eyes—
my father says we are a match."

Zilpah sees
blue—grayblue—seagray shadows—
violet slash of horizon
gulls circling a fisherman
rowing homeward—

The handmaid capsizes into Leah's arms.
Carried on the buoyancy of salt tears at last,
she sobs upon the rise and fall
of Leah's breast.

XXVII

The lamp Jacob cups in his palm
ignites Rachel's black eyes
as she offers her face.

Again her tense symmetrical gaze
squeezes the heart in his chest.
She looks away—a line of gold
curves from cheekbone
to closed lips, her laugh
hidden in the corners.

When she raises an arm to lift
the weight of dark hair from her forehead

he is unbearably aroused.
And his arousal fills her with a turmoil
she transforms to dance

crosslegged on the wedding sheet
flushed and stirred
she knows her breasts rise as she uncoils her hair,
sways in place to the flute and drum,
spreads her knees as she had swayed alone
on her sister's marriage night:
Leah, Jacob, be thou my wife, my husband. . .

Breath is choked from her—
Jacob kisses her mouth, eyes
and breasts—
The curling wool of his beard
strangely soft, herb-fragrant,
smothers, and yet she does not die—

There is no part of her
that his body does not enter
in every part a scream
rises like scald

"Rachel........Deceiver.........Betrayer"
Like a litany
chanting
thrusting

The scalding scream
overflows

a terrifying shudder
long diminishing sob

Whose are the tears on their faces?

She has forgotten Leah.

Part Two

XXVIII

By the door of a doubled house
Four women work to one loom

Bilhah sings: *Who created the day / the night?*
                      Nammu, her surging waters.
                      Who rises with the light?
                      Enlil, the god of air.
                      Who opens with the night?
                      Inanna, goddess of love.

Cutting with sharpened stone
Four women work to one loom

Zilpah sings: *No hands created the day*
                      but fins of Astroklas and Cet—
                      the great sea serpents leaping—
                      fire of his nostrils the sun
                      fire of her tongue the moon.

Tightening perfect knots
Four women work to one loom

Leah sings: *A breath created the light*
                      turning the darkness under.
                      Yahweh breathes in the night
                      and clouds are blown from stars.

Weaving the symbols of days
Four women work to one loom

Rachel sings: *He called the light Day*
and the darkness Night.
What is day without plowing of field?
What is night without setting of yeast?
Hands of men and women
perform the risen day.

XXIX

Days of rain.
Odors of fertile earth.
Muzzles graze windless pasture
sheltered by the high northern ridge.
Warm haze fills the bowl of this field
with spice of chervil,
wild onion, blue thyme.
Jacob rests his back
against dry outcrop,
takes from his pouch a gauzewrapped
chunk of hardened cheese,
barley bread, and now—
                          a stem
starred with red juice berries reaches
for his fingers through a crack
in bare rock—
                    small miracle,
gift of the god who may not be named,
and Jacob blesses this rock
with a name,
Stone-That-Bears-Fruit.

XXX

The days of Jacob open and fold
in the arms of Rachel.

Leah rounds with child,
blessing of the bridal week,

but Jacob looks away.
"His hate swallows my soul—

though he wants no part—"
Leah whispers to her handmaid

whose seagray eyes
mirror furies of the forsaken,

"and the husk remains—
here—just below the heart—

can you feel it with your hand—
it crowds the unborn. Zilpah,

shall such be his son—a stone
without voice or tears?"

XXXI

Yet Jacob sees the form
of Leah's ripening
round as the jug of milk she bears
lightly upon her head
as she climbs the sloping path.
Her garment swings with joy
over limbs still quick and slim.

A fragment of his soul
has escaped to the keeping
of her womb.
Something of the sun's implacable fire
has ignited her flesh.
He shields his eyes,
dares not gaze into the blinding will
of the absolute One—

Shall flame be the color
of his first son?

XXXII

The village tents and claywalled houses
lower their roofs in homage
to Laban's brick doorway
shaded by male and female fig trees.

His hearth warms the household gods—
ancestral teraphim
through generations of wandering

with small herds seeking
fallow pastures,
building no houses

until Betuel, Laban's father,
named these oak woods and hills
golden with edible grasses

sown by accident of winds. Here,
the people of Laban's tribe,
houseborn, or money-bought from a foreigner,

plant in measured rows,
nightly enclose their animals,
live, work, increase, as dwellers in Aram.

XXXIII

Kicked by a goat's hoof, a stone
ricochets, bruising her sandalled heel.
A bluish sickle moon
floats in barren twilight.
A trickle of monthly flow
stains her groin.

As a boy might do, Rachel
picks up the stone
and hurls it at the sky's hated
ghost calendar:

Plant lentils at the full
wheat at the dark
barley under the horn
Plant a son
as the husband wills

XXXIV

With mortar and pestle, Bilhah
crushes dried membrane saved
of sheep's ovary together with
flowering herbs and red emmer kernels.
The Sumerian handmaid scoops
yolk clusters from cut-up hens,
adds the unborn eggs to broth.
She bakes for her mistress
freshly dug turnip roots
round as birthing bellies.

Yet Rachel does not conceive,
she must endure the season's
overbursting smells of milk,
fermenting curds, molds of butter,
cheeses like hardened swollen breasts
bandaged in gauze.

XXXV

The milk-cow lows,
wide horns rip the air—
Atoning with soft words—for she knows
her hands had clamped like jaws on the teats—
Leah restores familiar rhythm—

Yet a second pain
embraces Leah's back like iron arms
of a form that presses,
constructed of pain, wanting
to become Leah.

Now a searing doubled yoke
grips from spine
around to belly

pulling her downward
to her knees.
The sling of her muscle
propels the child
slowly.

XXXVI

Firmly in orbit, the moon
observes the birthing tent
pulsating
six-poled star.

Midwife Meyaledet unrolls a reed mat
woven light as veiling
over spongy meadow grass
and dried leaves.

The heat of Leah's labor glows
in a film of moisture
on the other women's faces.

Meyaledet walks with Leah
chanting
to rhythms of contraction
widening
the tunnel of flesh
the child must learn to swim.

Voices of Zilpah, Rachel, Bilhah,
ullulate sounds of flowing water
as Meyaledet sings
the journey of Leah's child:

> *ah now the pain is your ally*
> *ah now you gather your breath*
> *ah now the tunnel widens*
> *ah now the walls embrace*

XXXVII

Now Leah lies on her side,
now she rears upward,
pants as the waves surge

as women's hands
move in circles upon her back
cooling the friction
with minted powders

The midwife's hands must hear
the heartsound
flutter of a water bird
dipped and turned
by pounding river banks
listen
to belly   pelvic bone   vulva
Meyaledet's hands must see
in the dark

Rachel with cool moist linen
wipes sweat from the laborer's forehead

But Leah rises
high on her knees
to the crest of her first great push—

butts her head in the air
free of her sister's touch.

XXXVIII

The shape of the laboring abdomen
subtly changes
as an underground river rising
shifts the contours of a hill

The child's head slides
forward into the web
moves back
and forward on another surge

Meyaledet's fingers hear
the lung-beat swimming
out of dark moons of water

into the first harsh suck
dust   air

XXXIX

ah now push
ah now push

still Meyaledet sings
to Leah's last laboring

> *ah now the sweet head*
> *ah now sweet shoulders*
> *ah now sweet cord*

"Ah-ah-ah—"
the wail of the newborn
cuts sharp through the songs

Leah gazes at the child
whose perfect lips and tongue
guided to her nipple
suck with faultless mastery

She names him Re-uven /
See: a Son!

XL

Jacob does not dare to touch
the heart's fountain
pulsing within his son's skull

Opening the swaddling cloth
he counts the marvels
of translucent nails

eyelashes curving one by one
ruddy skin newly washed and oiled
the fine twin testicles

sexual member
suddenly erect
and Jacob laughs

from the depths of his chest and abdomen
as he has never laughed—
laughter that radiates

in chorale throughout his household—
the sounds of laughter
of Jacob and his women

bell over the village
swirl like a cloud of praise
reverberating through the fields

deepened by the booming laughter

of Laban and the brothers of Leah—

"A son. . . . . .a son!"

The child's fists, tightly
grasping his father's
roughened thumbs,

will not let go—
and pulled by desire,
though his head wobbles back,

stands on the day he is born.

XLI

All the women know—
and none of the men—
that some pull of the moon
brings to harmony
blood cycles of women who live—
by love or force—
together in one house.

Jacob establishes rules:
because it is seemly,
because she bears sons,
he makes a husbandly division
to stay with Leah
one week out of four.

XLII

The wives of the village round and swell.
Leah's fourth son tongues his mother's nipple,
satiated lips bubbling.
His brothers wrestle in wild grass
like small animals

and run to their mother's sister
with prizes—morsel of honeycomb,
dove's egg, winged green insect—

Rachel tightens knots at the loom
and will not touch their grimy
dimpled fists or smile
into their shining
eyes dark as Jacob's.

XLIII

On a lone seventh night, Rachel
lights a spoonful of oil,
draws with a sooted reed
upon a square of cloth

the likeness of the god
Yahweh-without-a-face.
She draws a disc, its right half
rayed as the sun,
left half rippled as the moon.

Around the heavenly body,
dots, scratches—pairs of wings
of bird, butterfly,
moth, bat or fins of the flying fish
that leaps, Bilhah says, from central deep
to delta bank of the River Tigris.

Multitudes—
Souls beating—
Against the Sun/Moon—
Is this not Yahweh's face?

XLIV

"You may thank me, son-in-law,
for Leah's womb.
My youngest daughter
wastes your good seed.
Never mind—I am pleased with you."

It is true—
were it not for Laban's trick,
the sisters' complicit silence,
he would not be called *Jacob-
Father-of-Sons*,
would have no name in the village
other than Laban's nephew-slave.

XLV

It is always in the darkness
of wedding night betrayal
that Jacob comes into Leah, silent

mother of his sons.
The nightroom's air stirs
with moist sibilant breathing

youngest bedded in a ship of reeds—
woven by Leah's handmaid homesick for the sea—
older brothers upon their rug, a tumbled

litter of looselimbed foxes.
Those are Leah's marriage nights:
dark, breath, hidden spasm, silence, breath.

Perhaps the children,
on nights of the father,
conspire to mimic dreaming,

for on nights of the absent father,
they gather into the warm
mounds and burrows of Leah's humming flesh.

It is when they sleep,
say the grandmothers,
that children's bodies grow.

XLVI

Jacob's hands
ripple the lean nakedness of Rachel

in flickerings of lamplight
He loves to watch her drift

spent
shadows alive with her motionless form

as a tree mirrored on water
shatters at the touch . . . . . . reassembles

as grasses under flails of wind
return

quivering
still

XLVII

Half-aroused dreaming Rachel's upraised arms
braiding her hair into hard twin ropes,
he smiles, names her aloud: this time,

Rachel's arms bind his ribs in a vise:
"Jacob, I cannot bear my life!
Give me children—if not,
I will die!"

That he may not strike this woman
for the outrage of her tongue,
his fingers impress her wrists
as into coils of clay:

"Am I in place of Yahweh
who has denied you
fruit of the body?"

XLVIII

'Help me, Jacob—
my mother had no children
until she offered to
First Mother/First Father—after,

five sons were born to her,
then my sister and myself.
Come—help me
make an offering to the teraphim."

His hoarse whisper thunders in her ears
as once she heard hammering
horns of a ram trapped within a rock cave—

"Will you ask idols to put a child
in your belly?
Am I a foreign slave?
It is from Yahweh that I receive—
as free man, husband, father—
what I merit
or forfeit
of the herds that fatten and increase
according to my care.
By Yahweh's reward will I receive
descendants.
Let your father beg
blessings from dead skulls—
not I
nor you
nor any who belong to me!"

XLIX

Oracle faces:
ancient features
molded in plaster on skulls

of First Mother/First Father.
Below the carved forehead ridge,
eyes of agate

see their children's children.
They smell with honed nostrils
odors of fresh sacrifice,

taste with tongues of hearth flame.
In measured droplets,
Rachel's handmaid pours into the fire

milk of a fertile ewe veined
by a ribbon of her nursling lamb's blood.
The flames hiss, drink,

spit out pungent embers,
blackened stones.
Bilhah returns the teraphim

to their cloaks of linen
dyed with madder, saffron, murex.
Her secret burns to ordinary ashes.

L

Four turns of seven days
bring no kindness
to Rachel's cramping womb.

She forgets to lead the sheep
home to their evening fold.
Bilhah seeks her at the well

where Jacob, twelve years before,
had kissed her as cousin.
By the well, she waits

for her husband or another with bull strength
to shoulder the massive stone aside
that the animals may be watered.

Rocked in Bilhah's embrace,
Rachel, worn by thirst,
cannot weep.

LI

Is it mistress or slave who dreams
the moon unravels like a skein of thread

shining within a seamless cave?
Do both envision the loom at their knees,

as Bilhah's left hand guides, Rachel's right hand pulls,
luminous rows through night-black cloth?

Who counts the knots of red silk
to mark her turns of bleeding?

Light revolves in the hollow—
is it wife's or handmaid's thought

that reflects—like the moon—
the image of another's fire?

LII

In whose dream does the carved loom
grow from roots of cypress, a frame
broad as Jacob's shoulders,
with a crown of dust-green needles?
Through the warp of living sinews,
four women weave like vines
pliant, binding, thirsty.

The dream passes through the sighing
nest of Leah and her sons

encloses Zilpah's skin with salt

winds through a braid of Rachel's hair

seizes Jacob as he falls asleep beside her

draws Bilhah's knees to her crossed arms

LIII

Since unnumbered days of wanderings,
this is divine law:

> *No one may profane a woman*
> *inviolable by right of belonging*
> *to another man*
> *in blood, bond, or marriage.*

> *So, too, is the father's gift*
> *of a slavegirl to his daughter*
> *inviolate*
> *to any man*

> *except as her body may serve*
> *the woman who owns her labor.*

Rachel gives to Jacob
her handmaid, Bilhah,
that she may give birth
to Rachel's child.

LIV

No flute trills, no tambourine
shivers. The village bakes
flat customary breads.

Jacob lifts the curtain
of the handmaid's niche,
enacts a simple rite of seed
without thought of her name.

Bilhah's thoughts have flown
to a prince among stars
who leads her to a house
of cloud-blue lapis lazuli.
As he anoints her breasts
with fragrant oil,
in silence she sings remembered
words of the goddess Inanna
to her sacred lover Dumuzi.

LV

The slavewoman's crystal of honey
nibbled from the comb
melts in the mouth of her mistress.

Each sip of milk
or juice of fermenting grain
slakes another's thirst.

The hundred days' quickening
like the twitch of a straw
swells her womb

as though Rachel's fingers
hollow an offering bell of clay.
Yet

before the rooted seed
jabs with restless arms and legs,
crying *life* —

these days are the handmaid's
who curls in secret union
listening.

LVI

Night
like the blade of an axe
severs her bonds
                        Bilhah springs
through starless black
She gathers poppies that open in the dark—
reds, yellows more intense than those
shriveled by daylight

Her daughter, child of the night,
swims into her womb singing "Mother,
my name is Ashnan. . ."
goddess of grain

Let starved Rachel name any sons of Jacob—
She will have a daughter—

kindly and bountiful is she
who lives in a house
with Lahar, the shepherd god

LVII

"His name is Dan—
God has done me justice—"
cries Rachel
louder than the birthing woman's cry

On the boy's first scream
she raises him high in her hands
as Meyaledet cuts
and ties the slippery warm rope

as Bilhah expels the last of him
in afterbirth

Rachel spins in slow ecstacy,
"He has given me a son."

Part Three

LVIII

Abraham's knife, they say,
with the speed of a snake's tongue,
without pain or blood,
cut the foreskin of Ishmael,
his son
by Hagar the slave. On that day,

all the males of his household,
"houseborn or money-bought,"
were circumcised.

When Abraham's knife
cut the foreskin of Isaac eight days old,
the baby screamed.
"You see," said his father,
his name is Isaac
which means *He Laughs!"*

A woman cuts thread,
a chicken's throat—
her mind weaving cloth,
ladling stew.
She kneels beside water
beating love-stained linen and wool
clean upon pebbles.

A man learns—
with the patience of a woman—
the honing of blunt
obsidian   flint   copper
to articulate blade

clasping the hilt
like the hand of a brother.

When Isaac's throat lay pulsing
beneath the withered bramble of his father's beard,
the knife descending
halted,
a ram bleated,
the ropes about his wrists and ankles
slid off like snakes.

Fat and blood of the ram sputtered upon the altar,
Abraham's blade rested upon Isaac's damp curls.
The boy swallowed odors of burnt flesh,
smoke, like a soul, spiralling upward.

LIX

Naftali, eight days old,
Rachel's second son by Jacob out of Bilhah,
unswaddled, glows
upon the fringed carpet of circumcision
and dances frog-limbed greetings
toward the great faces
whose mouths chant as they swim
through warm ocean
tides of his will—

sucks in a cavern of lung-breaking air
rigid
choking on the surety of death
on a long wail propels his life forward
to final deliverance—
the scent of Bilhah's milk.

LX

The doubled house branches
under new thatch dividing.

Rachel has weaned Dan and Naftali,
her fingers dipped in freshly curdled
milk she draws each day
from the youngest speckled ewe.
Smacking her lips to open theirs,
she feeds spoonfuls of long-simmered barley gruel,
humming as their bellies round.
Yet her sons leap from the throne of her lap
to nuzzle Bilhah in sleep.

Leah's four sons in a separate room
kick with toughened feet
wrestling dreams.

Leah wakes upon her solemn bed,
rises to gaze at Zilpah.
The dreaming virgin mourns
beside a sputtering hearth. The last root
disintegrates to stench of wet ash.
"See what this girl has done!" her father says.

The flame of Jacob's lamp
slowly extinguishes
the curve of Rachel's slender abdomen,
pale nipple's moon,
his land and sky, his wife.

LXI

One woman weaves by the door,
fingers flying into landscapes.

Deserts guard Aram to the west
to the edge of the sea flooding

silt from the shores of Cyprus.
Sand mysteriously salt

scrapes massive table mountains
fissured like mummified groins

of ancient man-gods.
In the air, a hawk's wing cracks

twisting like an ankle
on a false betraying windcurrent. Leah's voice

calls slurred syllables of a name.
Zilpah's fingernails claw the fabric

before she rises, enters the tent
and waits for Jacob.

LXII

Now it is Leah who combs the Cypriot's hair,
kisses her mouth in a ceremony of smiles,
tempts her tongue with glazed cakes,
nuts mortared with poppy seed.
Slowly Zilpah's body conforms
to the hidden lump of clay—
Astet with gravid belly,
pendulous breasts.

Zilpah gives birth to a son, and bears again.
Leah names the first Gad / *Fortune* —
the second, Asher / *Happiness.*

It is told their eldest brother finds love apples—
now Leah may hire her husband back
from her sister. Jacob accepts
his bond, justice again—birthright
purchased by a sister for something to eat.

Leah gives birth to Issachar,
then Zebulun,
then Dina, seventh child,
first daughter.

Zilpah's fingers blur with speed at the loom
weaving patterns of Aram's desert
to the east, toward Shechem
in the land of Canaan.

LXIII

Rachel paces the stone rim of a well
with waters wider than earth—
How beautiful to walk the circumference
around the calendar of water—
the sky's true home—
each constellation a tribe,
each star, set in the pattern,
beating like a heart.

After nine changings of the moon,
she closes the circle
at the mossy print of her first step—
Why has she never seen this before—
all the constellations are held within the outline
of a woman's form   white wavelets
ripple the darkness floating
her loosened hair   bright oval
welcoming the reflection of her own face—

Into her mother's arms
Rachel dives—

Rising sun
follows them
downward

LXIV

Rachel wakes from a dream she cannot remember,
her eyes filled with reasonless tears.
These are, she decides, tears
of a true mother.   Therefore,
through the months of her pregnancy,
each day she weeps giving thanks

to Yahweh, to the features of his face
in the valley's rim of fissured mountains,
in spined desert bush, green wild flax,
sheaves of wheat at the edge of pasture,
tendrils of visible white breath
from nostrils of ewes grazing

and with arms cradling her abdomen,
shawl covering her hair,
she thanks the teraphim as well.

LXV

Rachel labors during a night of rain.
Beside houses and tents,
all cisterns upturned to the sky
fill with blessing.
Within the fold, drinking troughs brim over.

This is a night of births
among the animals—
by morning, seven ewes
lick the cauls from blind
trembling eyelids, limbs unfold
like broken sticks made whole.

According to custom,
no man enters the birthing tent—

but Jacob,
drops of rain scattering from his shepherd cloak,
eleven times a father—
for the first time, gazes
into the eyes of a newborn son. Motionless,
engraving each other's faces
on the tablets of their lives,
they hear Rachel's voice naming:
Joseph.

LXVI

Like small pharoahs, water birds
with sleek black heads
sail the river
risen from underground crevice

The rains have washed fragrance
of edible herbs as a gift
to all that breathes, pastures
overflow bare brown hills

Wind cleanses the outlines
of Yahweh's face
and the face of the child
who blooms with her milk

From this summit, Rachel and her husband
see herds resting by the well
where Jacob had watered her sheep—
"God has removed my reproach," she says

but Jacob turns in a circle,
at each turn tallying
fruits of twenty years as bondsman—
"The reproach was mine—for my fault

God closed your womb.
Not for me were Leah's sons,
or those born upon your knees by handmaids,
but as promise to my grandfather.

He gives us Joseph as a sign
I have at last deserved my father's blessing."

LXVII

Harsh cries hurry the clouds—geese ascend
pulled by invisible reins—
Hawks follow—

solitaries soaring as one migrating flock—
an arrow of eagles, doves, songbirds
flying toward Canaan.

Driven by winds of return, Jacob's herds
drum across the fields of Aram:
"Take nothing of Laban's—

these are my rightful wages." His sons race
to gird camels and donkeys to bear
rolled tents of Jacob's household.

Dina's hair,
that gleams black as Leah's and Rachel's,
whips in a single braid as she whirls the loom apart,

unhooks the moon and stars half-woven. The women
pack saddle bags of stitched goatskin,
cushion with bundles of herb the brittle

dome-baked bread, oils, cheese, dried dates,
figs, yellow tamarind—smells of citrus, sweat and dung
will deceive salt desert pillars

with memory of fertile field.

LXVIII

But one of Jacob's household strains against the wind.
Her child gleefully rides the basket she carries
above her bulge of new pregnancy.

There are others who fear nomad months
of leading thirsty flocks, each night
unfurling dusty tents. Many hoard amulet

spirits of root/branch, conception/birth.
At Laban's hearth, his daughter Rachel
unleafs ancient stiffened cloth from teraphim—

with eyes averted speaks their names *Mother/Father*—
cradles them on pillows of daily linen
hidden in a child's clean blankets.

When she seats the boy again,
he will not stay,
stubborn, he stamps the ground.

Rachel returns slowly, bent by the weight
of small gods huddled to her chest,
the other arm linked to Joseph's proud stumbling.

LXIX

wind at their backs   haze
  cloud motes of grit
mountain crags   carved shadows
   erosion   by dust   and by dust
restoring   earth rises
  from the hooves of oxen
settles in crevices

  eyelashes coated white, Rachel
breathes through her shawl
  wind at her back   mountain
a shrouded old woman's head
  her mother's face   entombed
the eyelids of the wilderness
  fall in folds   naked forehead sags
deep wrinkle across the bridge
  nose pulls toward crumpled mouth
lipless   cheeks a mass of veined furrows

  can this be the face of her mother
  who died giving her birth
  do the entombed young
  grow old   wizened skin
  aging the face of the earth

  Joseph sleeps as the basket rocks
  the camel's thudding gait   slow
  as rain on his birthing tent
  Rachel had carried him unborn
  into dream of unending water

dust risen from hooves of oxen
shaken from cracked slopes
dust of her face sifted into the haze
this child journeys in a parched womb

LXX

First, there was light—therefore
at midday, for one blinding instant,
perfect fire wheels to heaven's apex
consuming shadow: nothing

created of earth, whether
so delicate as a moth's hair,
may cast the dark of its being
upon any other fragment.

In Yahweh's sun, Jacob's and Laban's furies
burn as two equal in right.
"If any one of mine shall have stolen
your teraphim,
that one shall not live."

LXXI

Her father's shadow unravels the tent's
woven door, yet Rachel does not rise.

Laban waits, fingers coarsened by prodding
sides of every bundle, prying basket and jar
while daughters, servants, children
flowed from his path like water into the ground.

In the dimness, light sifts evenly
upon the burly grizzled pursuer
and his youngest daughter who sits,
wrapped in a wide cloak the colors
of dusk. The black moons of her eyes
reflect her father's temper.

The tent walls sigh—translucent
forms of two women
frame his daughter as in a doorway,
motionless, gazing at Rachel with eyes
curved in graceful resemblance.

       Laban is not a man
out of time, given to visions—yet he knows them
as his flesh and bone—
as the wife of his youth, Rachel's mother—
as Rebecca, his sister, mother of Jacob—

Only the dead pass through walls—
why do they gaze at his daughter?

Rachel, seated upon saddle cushions,
sees only her father's astounded eyes,
and says, "Forgive me
if I do not rise,
for the time of women is upon me."

LXXII

Mirage dissolves. . . .three women
shimmer into one. . . .the bones of Rebecca
and First Rachel

take possession of his daughter's face
rigid   white
as skulls of teraphim.

The touch of a menstrual woman
drains lifeblood.
Invisible

demons   leeches
servants to women's moons
bloat drunken

mouths clamped
to the man's heart.
"Daughter," Laban says,

"women's bodies bleed out of spite.
I will leave your tent—
which belongs to me—

and with your husband
cut a final covenant."

LXXIII

On the eastern bank of the wadi
at the Jabbok crossing
rise a hundred tents,
pegs soundly hammered—
a village sprung up in wilderness,
fires of dried thatch and dung
crackling, air thick with smoke
and cries of scolding mothers
sharp as barking yells of the herders.
The cattle's grit-scratched nostrils
sniff water foaming from nowhere
down the dry crevasse.

Jacob, cloaked in sheepskin,
content that all have safely crossed,
alone upon the western rim,
gazes upward.

As though someone stands on the eastern bank
with the sun at his back, a shadow,
like thongs of silhouette pulled across,
slowly bridges the Jabbok gorge,
denying the path of the sun
sinking in the west.

Tonight, constellations descend.
Lion is brilliant—half-beast,
half-man—stalking Snake
who bursts her skin showering scales
beyond the magical rod—
hunter's bow   shepherd's staff   royal sceptre
inlaid with bluewhite fires

each light an eye by which divine
beings pierce the thoughts of creatures
bound fast in dream.

LXXIV

A pregnant woman must not kill
so much as a gnat:
the spirit of death set free
might hover on gauze wings.
Rachel, asleep, flicks her hand—
a whining shiver
pauses
returns
stings
"Sister!"

In the adjacent tent, Leah, half-dreaming,
turns her strong hips sideward to stand.
Her hair, lit by strands of gray, flows
past the rise/fall
of her daughter's peaceable breathing.

Dina wakes chilled, blanket slipped
too far.
Outside, across the Jabbok gorge,
frost gleams as though stars
have shattered upon the stone rim.

At a baby's glottal warning of loud cry,
she bends quickly to the entrance
of the tent where Rachel and Leah
sleep, hair woven into one braid,
each listening to dreams of the other.

Dina's scent of flushed youth
infuses Joseph's milky warmth

as the girl becoming woman
rocks her half-brother
to whispered song.

The first rooster crows
and another—
calls of triumph
intensify
sounds of footsteps
coming
steps of a stranger
foreign   crippled
the tent flap trembles
Dina screams
a man
stained with sweat
and luminous dust

Like wings of a mother eagle
the arms of Leah and Rachel
circle to clasp the virgin
holding her brother.

"Is it Jacob?"
Rachel asks.
"Not Jacob.
My name is Israel:
God-Fighter."

LXXV

According to age
they sit:
a dagger's curve of youths

tough as desert palms
rooted in stony ground

ten sons of Israel
clenched fists imperceptibly
enacting
            jabs
   twists
       holds

their father's story of the night:
as lion against bull
hour after hour
neither giving way
sundown through dawn

they listen:
brothers, half-brothers
bitter with jealousy
teeth biting on hunger
taut muscles craving

birthright:
to wrestle
Yahweh's messenger
each to receive
his chosen enemy

LXXVI

Who are ten sons of one father?
     Born of Leah: Reuven, Simeon, Levi, Judah,
                      Issachar and Zebulon
     Born of Bilhah: Dan, Naftali
     Born of Zilpah: Gad, Asher
By whose wish are they named?
     Each is named at birth by a woman
Is their father just in his love?
     Not one receives a blow of his fists
     Not one the salute of his lips
What is the name of their sister?
     A swirl, a braid, a syllable
     Flick of tongue to the teeth
Who is eleventh, a golden cub, sleek
In their father's arms?
     Born of Rachel:
     His name is a burr in their throats
     Choked with longing

LXXVII

After weeks of dry forage,
Jacob's herds savor crushed green stems.

Almonds blossom beyond the houses and tents
of Shechem in the land of underground rivers

hospitable for pasture, trade, rest
for Rachel and her unborn child.

Her face grows gaunt on the journey,
limestone white.

Only Meyaledet knows she pads herself,
staining untimely,

as though the lie told to her father
becomes, in retribution, truth.

LXXVIII

At the instant before dawn stains the white
webs that shroud prickly hedges

Meyaledet skims the tatters,
excellent for stanching blood. Dina

follows her mentor, discerning odors of herb,
colors of henna leaf, pollen,

forked or nubbed shape of root
to be dried and pounded, or to ferment,

filter slowly in the manner of silt
washing to delta loam.

Slender as Rachel in youth
and with the same flare of fire in her limbs,

Dina's glances soothe with sea-gray
nurturing stillness

born of her mother, Leah.
Acquiring midwives' art, Dina's fingers

probe the soil, blind and wise as earthworms
weaving threads of life

where light would kill.

LXXIX

The dream-terror begins
paralyzed throat
screaming endless silence

Mouth open
Dina trembles awake

No dream, the ancient wall
of costly burnt bricks
inscribed, he says,
with the names of his fathers
unto generations of fathers

In the house of Shechem
where he had placed his hand
like a bronze slave circlet
about her throat

His handsome braggart teeth
numbing her lips

and she cannot scream
as the thick barbed club
claws
rends
beating until

rasping
shudders
spills
blood
defiling her

LXXX

Her fault—bite her tongue—
curse the women of Canaan.

Our virgins are taught
not to stare, bold, at a man.

What a fool—our prince
begs the Hebrew piece for his bride

and to marry her wet blue eyes
he will slice off the skin of his tail

all of them—from princes to diggers
of graves—
will maim their own members

and to marry their camels and goats,
they will force us to marry their men

cram foreign wives into our beds
and send our daughters
to lie among strangers in tents.

A girl accustomed to brothers—
is that any reason to look
without fear into faces of men?

LXXXI

Jacob/Israel, *God-Fighter*,
lifter of stones,
cannot wrest the blooded club
from his daughter's wound.

Before him, the fissured stone hills.
Behind him, pasture darkening
with idle patterns of shadow.
Above, clouds drift,
sky clear, mute.

Should not the stones find voice,
cry out to the heavens?
Only the lowing of cattle ascends,
bleating of sheep.

Yet a sound as of veils sweeps
over fields,
as of grasses rustling,
water bubbling from hidden springs

echoes
openthroated ullulations

the women of the family of Dina
stand
left hand to the right of one
right hand to the left of another
echoing

through the valley of Shechem
swirl of their voices seeking
the chamber

where Dina
listening
lifts her arms
the stains of her swaying body
cleansed.

LXXXII

No clay tablet
in the fires of the pillaged city
records the bridal pact:

how Hamor and Shechem
and every male of the city
submit to the blade
of circumcision
for marriage right, exchange
of wives and properties.

Would the pricks of a stylus matter
or the imprints of thumbnails?
Could not a tablet shatter
at the blow of a sword
no less than the raw flesh
of unmanned warriors?

With their plunder of animals,
gold, weapons, widows and orphans,
Dina's brothers

carry her past the corpses
of Hamor and his son
past bricks inscribed with the names
of the fathers of Shechem—

And to Jacob, their father,
outraged at the reek of their deeds,
they answer in words
told by the scribes:
"Should our sister then be treated as a whore?"

LXXXIII

Through sunblessed meadow
Jacob leads his people
bearing jars of water-from-stone
that springs clear
as the ladder-of-light
dreamed in his youth
at Bet-El / *House-of-God.*

He breathes the stolen fragrance
of Esau's garments, hears Isaac's voice:
See, the smell of my son
is like the smell of a field
that Yahweh has blessed.

The cloaks of Jacob's sons
reek with the fetid smell
of slaughterers' rags.

One by one, all of Jacob's household
file into their tents
to pour upon themselves
purifying waters
change their garments

and one by one
cast before his feet
all foreign gods

amulets   pendants   clay
figures of the-one-of-many-names
bigbellied, hands lifting her breasts,
and talismans of bone,
earring with face of a goat,

ivory lotus, hawk, sphinx,
and ancient teraphim
shrouded in linen.

All these Jacob buries
beneath the oak
whose knuckled branches
rap the scorched gates
of the city of Shechem.

Caressing her bowed head, his hand
perfumes the tent
with essence of balsam, myrrh
and frankincense
poured in offering
upon a standing-pillar
in the holy place, Bet-El.

His voice echoes the rumble of the stone lid
obedient to his young strength
opening the well
where she had come to water her father's sheep.
Jacob says, "I have again seen God."

The child within her
seems to hear, to dance
exultant kicks causing
blunt stabs of pain.

Rachel lifts her eyes, worn, questioning.
Jacob sees again
the luminous river of his love.
"Jacob, tell me
how to see Yahweh's face—
which mountain's shadow
draws his profile,
which stars the shape of his eyes?
Does rain sound the timbre of his voice,
shall I hear words in thunder?"

"Not thunder, nor whisper
of a grain of sand.
Yahweh has no voice,

God has no face,
yet I have heard his voice
and I have seen his face."

LXXXV

Jacob's caravan stretches toward Efrat,
a travelers' crossing-place,
water, pasture, rest.

Carried on the gentlest of the flock,
Rachel leans her heaviness forward
to ease
the donkey's jolting,

her mount paced on either side
by Leah and Bilhah

followed by Dina and Zilpah
abreast with Meyaledet

watchful
the midwife's cry rings out

birthing waters
gush from Rachel's womb.

LXXXVI

As women raise the six-poled star
of the birthing tent

time surges into pain
pain made of thirst
dry craving
her mother's arms receding

rim of the great well
contracting

pain that swallows the root
of herb called kindness-to-women
gathered at full moon by midwives

tensile root for strong contractions
oil pounded from its core
stroked on a knotted abdomen
releasing

pain blind to the light
dark   day   night
her mother's arms opening
invisible   where is the well
for her thirsting

For those who count brightness/shadow
three days/three nights
Jacob does not sleep

Rachel's voice burns away

like straw in the fires
heating broth
like particles of smoke
that obscure the lamps
lit in the birthing tent

Through the rhythms of women chanting
and the clear light song
of Dina-Gifted-in-Healing
the midwife's delicate skill
cannot turn the child in the womb
as he kicks   breeches forth
yet her hands battle the cord
that it may not become snake
to strangle at birthing

Rachel's voice a straw
burning to ashes   *ah   ah   ah*
the women singing
>   *ah now the pain understands*
>   *ah now do not be afraid*
>   *ah now for you comes a son*

covered with blood   a warrior face
the new son chokes

and wails
for his mother

who whispers
"Name him Ben-oni / *Son-of-My-Woe.*"

LXXXVII

According to custom
no man enters the birthing tent

but Jacob
lifts the light reed
of Rachel's wrist

to let the tips of her fingers
caress the pulsing
fontanel

and says,
"His name is Benjamin /
Son-of-the-Right-Hand."

LXXXVIII

In the cradle of a brief
afterbeat
the heart spins a warm
centrifugal
shudder to the limbs
and the sum of one
fastens into place.

Hands, voices, speak the ritual
scruples of the bath.
As in the washing
of a newborn,
threads of blood—the tangle of needs
from another life—
rinse into a basin.

They stroke in a single direction
from the nostrils
downward
from the armpits
outward
to clear all webbings of sweat
that cling to fingers
redeemed of fists.

And the touch
of the child born to earth
gives comfort
to the hands of its midwives.

LXXXIX

Her burial pillar stands
in a place
that knows no name other
than along-the-way
between Bet-El and Efrat.

One who serves as scribe
prepares a tablet of fresh clay
washed free of river sediments,
copies with reed stylus
from the marriage tablet
her name as Rachel
wife in perfect law
to Jacob son of Isaac son of Abraham
mother of Joseph
and Benjamin.

Into the disc of wet clay
three inscribe
the imprints of thumbnails:

a man's, like a stone pillar standing
a child's, like a seed of wheat
and one
might be
scale of a fish   petal   gnat's wing

XC

It is the earth that seems to move—
the village carried on its journey—

as though sheepfold, herds of cows,
goats, donkeys and camels,

many with nurslings,
and men, women, children,

mounted or on foot,
stand still, gliding in place

to follow the sun's destined arc,
though dust rises, step by step.

Charlotte Mandel is the author of *The Life of Mary*, a poem-novella (with foreword by Sandra M. Gilbert); *Doll*, a long poem published as a chapbook; and two collections of poems: *A Disc of Clear Water* and *Keeping Him Alive*. She coordinates the Eileen W. Barnes Award Series of first books by women poets over 40, and edited the anthology, *Saturday's Women* (coedited by Maxine Silverman and Rachel Hadas). As an independent scholar, she has published articles on the role of cinema in the life and work of the poet H.D. (Hilda Doolittle). Her awards include two fellowship grants from New Jersey State Council on the Arts; Open Voices Winner at The Writer's Voice in New York City; and residence fellowships at Millay Colony, Virginia Center for the Creative Arts, Villa Montalvo Center for the Arts, and Yaddo. Her 1989 residence at Yaddo was sponsored by the Geraldine E. Dodge Foundation. She was selected by New Jersey Business and Professional Women to receive the Woman of Achievement Award (field of the arts) in 1988. A dramatic adaptation of *The Life of Mary* was produced by Bill Bace Gallery, New York City, in May, 1990.